PATTERNS IN THE PSALMS

PATTERNS IN THE PSALMS

A colouring book

Illustrated by
James Newman Gray

First published in Great Britain in 2016

Society for Promoting Christian Knowledge
36 Causton Street
London SW1P 4ST
www.spck.org.uk

Compilation copyright © SPCK 2016
Illustrations copyright © James Newman Gray 2016

Verses from the Psalms selected and compiled by Juliet Trickey

British Library Cataloguing-in-Publication Data
A catalogue record for this book is available from the British Library

ISBN 978-0-281-07604-8

Typeset by Graphicraft Limited, Hong Kong
First printed in Great Britain by Ashford Colour Press
Subsequently digitally printed in Great Britain

Produced on paper from sustainable forests

This book belongs to

_____

INTRODUCTION

The Bible has always been a rich source of imagery; its stories and descriptions have inspired paintings, sculptures and stained-glass windows down the centuries. The patterns here find their origins in the Psalms, which speak of the wonder of creation and the glory of the God behind it all.

All the designs are based on the Bible passages included, focusing on either a theme or image in each text from the Psalms. Our prayer is that these verses will inspire your colouring and create a space for you to meet with God through Scripture.

Glorious are you, more majestic than
the everlasting mountains.

Psalm 76.4

More majestic than the thunders
of mighty waters,
more majestic than the waves of the sea,
majestic on high is the Lord!

Psalm 93.4

He it is who makes the clouds rise
at the end of the earth;
he makes lightnings for the rain
and brings out the wind from
his storehouses.

Psalm 135.7

Even the sparrow finds a home,
and the swallow a nest for herself,
where she may lay her young,
at your altars, O LORD of hosts,
my King and my God.

Psalm 84.3

The young lions roar for their prey,
seeking their food from God.
When the sun rises, they withdraw
and lie down in their dens.

Psalm 104.21–22

Let heaven and earth praise him,
the seas and everything that moves in them.

Psalm 69.34

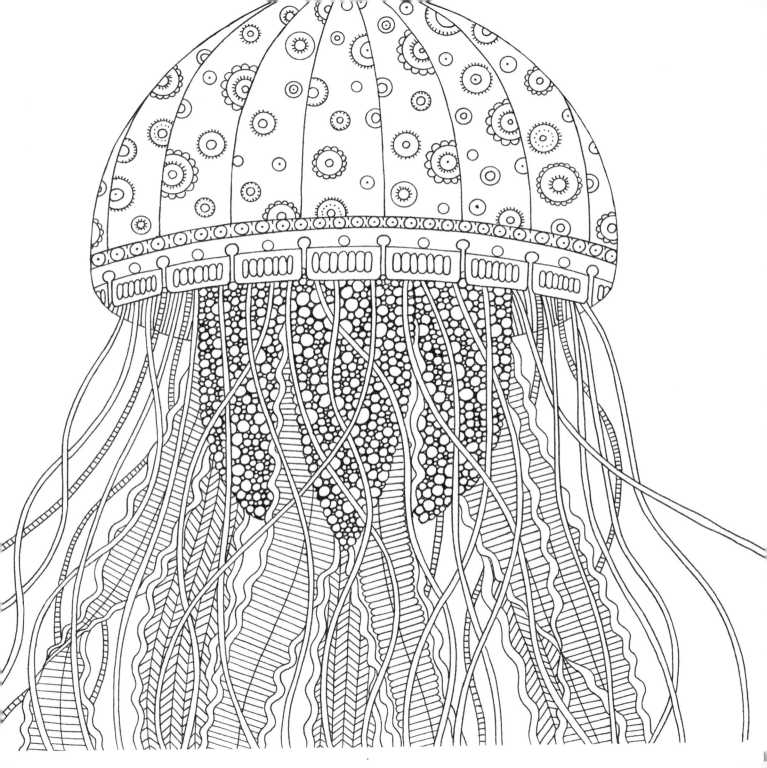

When I look at your heavens,
the work of your fingers,
the moon and the stars that
you have established;
what are human beings that
you are mindful of them,
mortals that you care for them?

Psalm 8.3–4

From the rising of the sun
to its setting
the name of the LORD is to be praised.

Psalm 113.3

You have fixed all the bounds of the earth;
you made summer and winter.

Psalm 74.17

Let the heavens be glad,
and let the earth rejoice;
let the sea roar, and all that fills it;
let the field exult, and everything in it.
Then shall all the trees of the forest
sing for joy before the LORD;
for he is coming.

Psalm 96.11–13

By the streams the birds of
the air have their habitation;
they sing among the branches.

Psalm 104.12

Sing to the LORD with thanksgiving;
make melody to our God on the lyre.

Psalm 147.7

The earth is full of your creatures.
Yonder is the sea, great and wide,
creeping things innumerable are there,
living things both small and great.

Psalm 104.24–25

You rule the raging of the sea;
when its waves rise, you still them.

Psalm 89.9

add detail to the waves

Therefore let all who are
faithful offer prayer to you;
at a time of distress,
the rush of mighty waters
shall not reach them.

Psalm 32.6

Happy are those who do not follow
the advice of the wicked . . .
They are like trees planted
by streams of water,
which yield their fruit in its season,
and their leaves do not wither.
In all that they do, they prosper.

Psalm 1.1, 3

The pastures of the wilderness overflow,
the hills gird themselves with joy,
the meadows clothe themselves with flocks,
the valleys deck themselves with grain,
they shout and sing together for joy.

Psalm 65.12–13

They sow fields, and plant vineyards,
and get a fruitful yield.
By his blessing they multiply greatly.

Psalm 107.37–38

Add your own patterns to the leaves

Your steadfast love, O LORD,
extends to the heavens,
your faithfulness to the clouds.
Your righteousness is like
the mighty mountains,
your judgements are like
the great deep.

Psalm 36.5–6

As a deer longs for flowing streams,
so my soul longs for you, O God.

Psalm 42.1

You have put all things
under [our] feet,
all sheep and oxen,
and also beasts of the field,
the birds of the air,
and the fish of the sea.

Psalm 8.6–8

Praise the LORD from the earth . . .
fire and hail, snow and frost,
stormy wind fulfilling his command!

Psalm 148.7–8

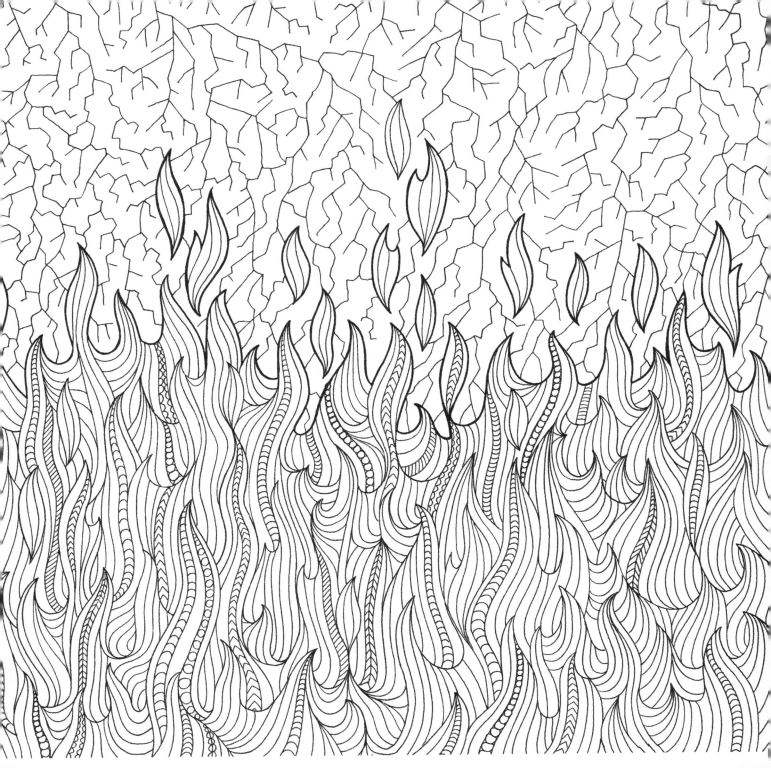

The mighty one, God the LORD,
speaks and summons the earth
from the rising of the sun to its setting.

Psalm 50.1

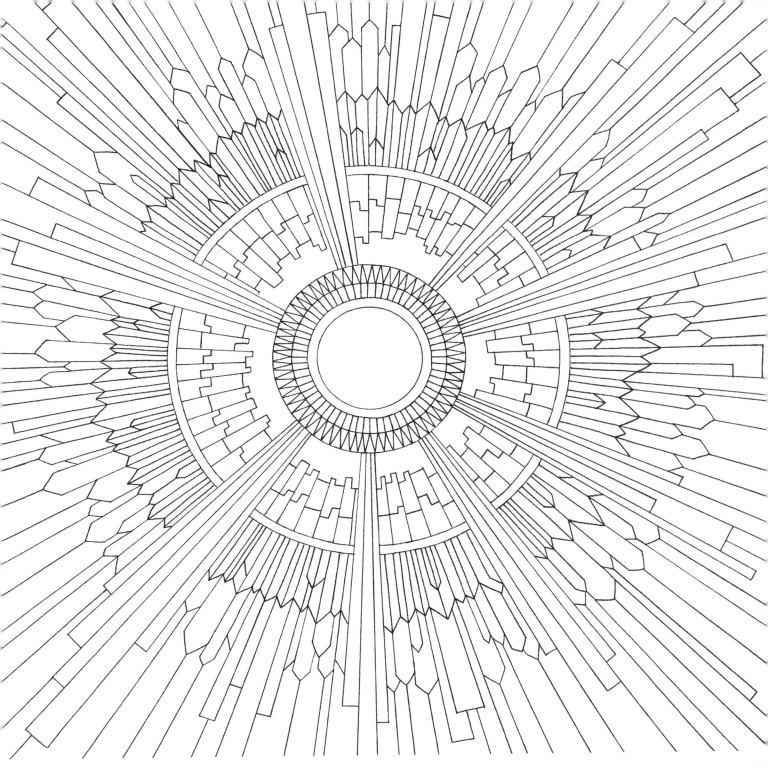

The fear of the LORD is pure,
enduring for ever;
the ordinances of the LORD
are true and righteous altogether.
More to be desired are they
than gold, even much fine gold;
sweeter also than honey,
and drippings of the honeycomb.

Psalm 19.9–10

Happy are those
who live in your house,
ever singing your praise.

Psalm 84.4

As far as the east is from the west,
so far he removes
our transgressions from us.

Psalm 103.12

He reached down from on high, he took me;
he drew me out of mighty waters.

Psalm 18.16

You are my hiding-place
and my shield;
I hope in your word.

Psalm 119.114

Praise him, sun and moon;
praise him, all you shining stars!

Psalm 148.3

Enter his gates with thanksgiving,
and his courts with praise.
Give thanks to him,
bless his name.

Psalm 100.4

Use your favourite Bible verse
as inspiration for your own design.

Printed and bound by CPI Group (UK) Ltd, Croydon, CR0 4YY

27/01/2025

14632680-0001